AF333550

Richard Hague

POSSIBLE DEBRIS

Cleveland State University Poetry Center
Cleveland Poets Series No. 43

ACKNOWLEDGMENTS

I wish to thank the editors of the following, in which these poems first appeared:

AMBERGRIS: "Old Fishing Lines"

APPALACHIAN JOURNAL: "City Gardens," "Black Sheep"

CINCINNATI POETRY REVIEW and CLIFTON: "House Cats"

GAMBIT: "Frost"

MOUNTAIN LIFE & WORK: "Fishing," "Giant Catfish, 1955"

PINE MOUNTAIN SAND & GRAVEL: "Mr. Washington," "Toward the End of a Long Ride"

RIVERWIND: "Penny"

SOAPTOWN: "Listening to Vivaldi While Watching Starlings Above the Railroad"

SHARED SYSTEMS: POEMS ABOUT LIVING WITH TECHNOLOGY, ed. Kezia Sproat for the Community of Poets Awards: "The Astronaut Looks Back at Earth," "One for Magnavox and Nietzsche"

TERMINÓ: "Slugs"

POETRY IN THE PARK, chapbook for 1983: "North To Fly By"

POETRY OHIO, ART OF THE STATE: AN ANTHOLOGY OF OHIO POEMS, ed. David Citino: "Limestone," "Root Fence," "Shore Glass, Cincinnati"

In addition, "Kneeling Down and Finding You've Forgotten How to Pray" is included with permission of the Sinclair Community College Writer's Workshop.

Finally, I am indebted to the Greater Cincinnati Foundation for a 1984 Teacher's Award Grant which greatly helped in the completion of this book.

Funded Through
Ohio Arts Council

727 East Main Street
Columbus, Ohio 43205-1796
(614) 466-2613

CONTENTS

A few years ago, the sculptor Claes Oldenberg was featured in a film broadcast on PBS. During a sequence shot in his studio, Oldenberg was asked where he got ideas for his work. Smiling, he made his way to the row of bins that ran the length of the wall. "I just come here," he told the interviewer, "and rummage around among this possible debris."

THE DOOR

Out of the gab and clatter
of the day, papers rustling
like the sound of brush fires
coming over the hill,
voices like bad weather
five miles off and closing,
radios blaring, spatter and honk
and stinking nudge of traffic,
I try to find the blue door
opening on silence.
I know it like a dream
carpentered of high desert sky,
its white knob polished bone
cool as winter to the touch.

Sometimes I watch myself
beginning to pass through.
In the middle of a word
I lean my weight against it,
fumble the latch,
and almost enter dissolving,
sidestepping in
between sun and decay,
between peace and the hard coming back.

HAULING GRAVEL FROM NEWTOWN

The pits are banked with sand.
Rich Miami topsoil wastes to smoke,
rides wind's gold dozer away.
All that's left is
dust of mountains, plowed moraines,
and this gravel, polished by ice's teeth
and the swirl of ancient waters.

Half a ton fits easily in my truck:
twenty thousand shards of Arctic,
displaced a quarter of a continent.

And now they move again,
southward on steel,
the blue fume of combustion,
the short hope of my project.

How have I come to this,
engaged in the labor of glaciers?
I, less than a moment in time,
dupe or accomplice,
uncertain among these old nomads.

LIMESTONE

Shell on tooth on bone, lime's
binding tight around them. No light:
a hundred fifty million years.
But watch, this common Tuesday in July,
the boy across Duck Creek
crack a flat slab open
and shout to see a fish
come blackly out of rock, chopping
with its teeth the strange and sudden sun.

Or elsewhere, by the Great Miami,
a rough-ridged, hand-sized stone,
dumped here years ago
from some high place in Ohio
once the delta of the Appalachian River.
Two hundred thirty million years.
And watch again: a young man on his knees
runs his fingers lightly down the ridges,
feeling roundworms in those lime-cast tunnels
thicker than his thumb.

Tooth entwined with bone entwined
with shell are bound together
in the dark of rock's hard time
until the hillside high above the creek
gives way, until the mountain breaks,
and ancient limestone bares its frozen moments
to the sunlight of our days,
while through the brilliant hollows
new waters scour and make clear
old time's shelled foundations.

KNEELING DOWN AND FINDING
YOU'VE FORGOTTEN HOW TO PRAY

The world is different down here,
its inhabitants lint and needles
and the snail-slow fading stains.

It is a quiet place whose only sound
is the deft spring of the silverfish
or the misery song of the roach.

The air seems stale and colder.
The sofa's sagging bottom shows its guilt.
There are no excuses.

Sockets leak electric like blank gargoyles,
flooding the rug with static.
What in hell can you do?

Strip bare the wires and bite them
and go down a sweat machine,
your eyes bleared inward with wild vision?

No. You listen to the beetle
in the floorboard making secret music.
You are caught up in its tune. You sing.

God hears you from the sweeper bag.
"Good boy," he says, "smart boy,"
and gives you dust to kiss.

BLACK SHEEP

Even to our mothers
we are strange.
Often first born, striking
and handsome as fire,
still we grow
birthday by birthday
more alien.
Like a hickory's bark
our natures turn rougher
each season.
Badgers grow meek
at our feet,
hawks shriek our names
over ridges.
When we marry —
if we ever do —
we find wild ones
of our kind,
red-eyed headbust women,
sisters of Lilith and dusk,
then drink ourselves
toward madness.
We are famous
in the fashion
of hurricanes, floods,
bad winters.
Those who remember us
cross themselves,
knock wood.
Nieces weep
when we glare.
Over our lives
shrikes and ravens

turn. Buzzards
uncover their heads
in our presence.
Earth sours
where we're thrown
at last.
Broom sedge
and knotgrass,
those seedy accomplices,
struggle to cover
our tracks.

SMOKE

Like my own blood kin, like a cousin,
smoke lived close,
hung from the cornices
of my neighborhood ridge
like the cloudy silk of spiders.
Together, we wormed our ways
deep into local caverns:
Sunshine, Rockledge, Fox's Den.
No matter how far, how deep,
we always went together.

And we were there, on the smoldering
gob heaps and brush-fired knobs
with the red-faced firemen, shouting,
a gang of black-handed boys.
And the brooms that we beat out those fires with
raised a dusty hell,
and my cousin.

Together, we grew wild,
painting ourselves
with our own special tints:
smoke with its graphite grays
and coke-smelted ochres,
I with my copperas creek yellows
and the scarlet of ragged split chins.
Over trash-fires in the gullies
we swapped breath,
as boys swap blood from a cut,
and camped all night
in the same smoldering places.

Now my breath has grown shorter,
but smoke's is twenty years stronger.
It hangs around town,

familiar as the mayor,
rich as the old Wheeling Steel.

When I go back home
for a visit, I remember
how close we had grown:
even in those days,
long before I fled, not knowing
what I fled,
smoke's trouble
was my trouble.

It still is.

THE ASTRONAUT LOOKS BACK AT EARTH

Halfway to the moon,
fetal in his womb of tube,
teletype, and wire,
he looks back
through a port no larger
than his daughter's face
to see the home place
laced like a farmhouse window
with its common curtains
of clouds.

Behind the memory
of lift-off,
launch control's dry voices
sparking in his helmet,
the temporary burden
of a dozen gravities,
he feels, within his
blood's intense and quick adventure,
a reminder that he is
somehow absent
from himself.

And he knows
that wherever he will have been,
he will return
home-hungry,
to flush again from his spacesuit
the delicate flesh
that he is,
to reincarnate himself
in the air-swaddled world
he was born to,
where a mouse still rummages
the pantry,

where his pants still hang,
smelling of grass,
on the bedpost,
where the cat's shadow still glides,
earthbound,
along the white garage.

NORTH TO FLY BY

In homing pigeons' brains
small lodestones
hang in webs of nerve:

This is where you go,
says every mountain to them
with its metal veins,
says every river
grinding ore dust
from its valleys,
is where you go,
says every iron-stained
sandstone ridge.

Far below,
night blanks landmark,
water-course, and range,
but steered by
charged and ancient earth
nothing can forget:

even new-moon minnows
trapped in down creeks
gather,
polished needles
pointing
this is where you go.

GIANT CATFISH, 1955

After catching shad as neat as gloves,
hand-sized from the Easter shoals
along the river's sloped sand,
I saw those catfish brooding monstrous
at the mouth of Yellow Creek one day.
Grandfather pointed toward
their thick trunks, prehistoric,
long as mammoth bones.

How many years of minnows
filled their cold bushel stomachs,
how many eight-inch smelts
cast out by dreamers
up from Steubenville?
And worse, how many boys?

Eight years old, I looked down
on their being,
idle power hardly moving
near the Water Works,
and measured how I'd fit
if somehow, for my sins,
I would tumble from the creek-wall
to their taking.

Days later, back at school,
I fled the Bible story
of the outlaw
swallowed by a whale.
All day I hunkered
in the blackest basement corner
as the nuns cast from their ghostly shores
accusing endless lines,
baited with my name.

PENNY

It was your fur gave
you that name: burnished copper,
smooth, a slick metallic sheen.
The first three weeks
I fed you by hand,
excited by the glimpse
of lean white teeth
between the slit of your nose
and lip.
I loved to stroke
your ears:
I admired how you laid them
back along your neck
like wings.

I was fourteen.
The world was large,
part of it named Girl.
I forgot you
for three days,
lingered after school
at Mosblack Grocery
for a whiff
of Brenda Royce's hair.

One late night of snow
I returned to your pen by the shed.
I found you stiffly stretched,
feed-bowl empty,
beautiful ears awry,
brown eyes wide
and frozen.
I saw blood on your claws,
scraped wood in the corners.

I could not touch you.
With my father's garden spade
I tilted you out,
rolled you over and
over
toward the compost pile.
A long dark settled after that.

Now a January evening,
traffic loud in a city
twenty years away.
A blaze of store-front light
glints in a woman's
penny-colored eyes:
I feel a delicate alien bone,
thin as a girl's brittle laughter,
suddenly sharp at my heart.

A PICTURE OF MYSELF, AGE FOUR, WEARING A GINGHAM SKIRT

Breeze billows it, the skirt
wide and round as an overturned cup,
while I, as if balanced on its top,
lean slightly to the right.

Strange: I am beautiful,
white-blond hair an unsteady
shimmering above my eyes,
a halo of tongues dancing.

What am I thinking?
What does any of us, this
perfect with youth, luminous
with health, ever need to think?

Are we all, once in our lives,
engulfed as in a harmless fire,
captured in a photo vivid with summer,
esplanades of elms and birdsong

opening everywhere beyond us, haze
a promise of wonder in the distance?
Once again, I try to gather
from this picture the feeling

of a body no larger than a pup's,
the adventure of my girl-cousin's clothes,
a thoughtlessness as sweet
and small as a violet's.

I remember nothing of it. Nothing.
My friends who see this picture
are startled from speech.
They hold it reverently at its edges,

relic, image from another world.
Wonder vanishes. They grow older
as I watch. I think they grieve.
Later, over drinks in the yard,

small talk hobbled, weakened
by time's mute, frank deposition,
they ask, uncertainly,
"Was that really you?"

What can I answer? What can we bear to hear?
For a moment all around us, the evening
is young, intense, and pure:
impossibly still.

MR. WASHINGTON

After the second green snake incident,
Mr. Washington required
my mother's promises — her full
cooperation. No way he'd
haul junk from that shed
with snakes in cages on the floor.
"No trash man got to be bit
to make a living."

I remember
watching from the backyard
as he said that, remember
how he shivered, swabbed his
thick arms with bandannas,
firmed his hat the closer
over dark eyes.
Fear in grown-ups was of interest.

Next time, I half-covered them
with tarps. Seven dynamite boxes
salvaged from the High Shaft mine,
newly primed with corn snake,
queen snake, racer.

"Mam, that dog don't hunt,"
was all he said to mother.
All summer, the rubbish built:
congeries of broken hoses,
half a roof's old shingles,
a burnt-out hornet's nest.

Next time was the charm.
Before the dark shed's door I stood
draped in coiling serpents: rat snakes
twined around my calves,

pilot blacksnakes hanging
from my shoulders,
puff adders flattened, hissing
at my feet.

Six weeks it took,
that trash.
Handload by sweating handload
under mother's eye
I had to haul it
to his pickup safely down the road.

But six weeks' education:
foot on bumper, stern and deep of voice,
Mr. Washington scowled and preached me:
how the hoopsnake to escape the farmer
rolls swift across the pasture, or
cornered, swallows itself down
to nothing —
"That there's what you're worth, boy" —

how every serpent
is a seedling of the devil's tail,
springing up in muck
scorched by lightning strikes,

how even God himself, that
ancient trash man
rummaging foundations,
piling odds and ends toward a world,
packs a keen hoe blade or case knife
to hack at evil,
or to skin him out, when he's hungry,
some smart-mouthed boy or two.

SOMETHING YELLOW

Here it is again, rising in a dream
of Walker's oily pond, that poisoned sink
below the cornfield
the cows came home from moaning.
Again aboard that torched-off cartop
that I poled across its sunboiled stench,
my feet and trouser-bottoms
slick with filth,
I sway sea-sick in the old Ohio
of my boyhood,
and see, my breathing quickened, shallow,
something yellow moving
just beneath the surface,
a grooved, humped egg-shape,
a living bloat and squirm,
drifting up
before me.

Again I do not speak of it
to those ashore,
my friends, boys wild with adolescence,
their grinning faces smeared with frog's blood
and scum of ransacked minnows;
in my dream it still is danger,
terrible and private,
sickness birthing in my world.

Nor have I ever, waking year after year
into the jumbled barricade
of reason,
recovered safety in my thoughts:
in all yellow, even in the innocence
of dresses worn by laughing sisters,

the brilliant milk truck
turning down the street each morning,
I feel again that strange confusion,
paralysis, constriction,
that fear of some unnamed other
living vividly, too close,
to what I thought was home.

FISHING

The Morse of man and beast,
a kind of wired connection:
the short then long of tug, release, then
shrill of line gone taut,
blood fevered at the touching.

Blood fevered at the touching:
that, elsewhere, in another life,
is passion's stunning wireless,
a Jacob's Ladder
blue and intimate
connecting flesh and flesh:
heart's spark from fingertips
conducted to the pulse-place
on her neck —
a questing, hunger for connection.

A questing, hunger for connection,
is what I suffer every hour
by this river, where
the heron reads the semaphores of light
flashed by schooling shad,
then leans, intent,
one-minded,
to spear the single fish he's eyed
from all the others.
But it's a different, gentler questing,
different hunger for connection
that I cannot turn away from,
each day remembering the girl
who at fifteen drowned
off Steubenville,
but never was forgotten.

She never was forgotten:
I linger daily by the river,

listening through thumb and index for the tap
tap code of nibble.
Tensed,
I look around,
confused in memory's mixed desire,
but in water's flash
see no arcing of her
up from stone or swirl of water,
see only
blonde leaves tattered
in the grounded roots of willows,
see only dying minnows, belly-up,
as swollen as her fingers,
flay shoreward in the spun gray scum
below the roaring mill.

CITY GARDENS

1

April's first full spade
along the driveway:
Zanesville brick, old granite
from some long-dead lawyer's birdbath,
sandstone bedrock of the hillside
graded for the college
fifteen years ago;
last year's walnut husks,
weed roots, a clump or two of clay.
Still, the work feels real,
holds promise.
A load of peat, some compost,
a dust of lime, we hope,
will do.
In a low branch of the locust,
a grackle's bronzes glow.

2

The neighbor's German shepherds
perch like sphinxes on the top step
of his porch.
They are not grinning,
but they seem to be.
We have watched them skid
through seedlings for the striped cat
fat with birds,
snuff the tender flames of beansprouts
with their urine.
Beyond the gray garage,
robins dab the bluegrass for slim grub.

3
Through five such afternoons we pass
from hope's grace to the shabby real
of blasphemy. We curse
the old elm stump whose roots
run like a vein of lead
beneath proposed tomatoes,
then swerve, impervious as slate,
beneath the onion bed.
Students linger, grinning,
watch a while,
then, shaking heads,
drift off, armed with frisbees
to teach physics to the air.

4
Peas, spinach, onions.
Their tastes live rich already
on our tongues.
At night, we wake
to fears of frost,
then slip off again,
lulled by the far drone of the freeway,
to dream of gardens long as rivers
winding into harvest's fertile coves,
where healthy, sunburnt,
we become the perfect persons
we have neglected all our lives,
and lean on hoes
like the old hands
we have heard of —
all for free.

SOLANUM

Borne to his birth in a sack
among brothers nudging and silent,
he has his kind's protuberant, quizzical features.
He reads the ground like a book,
masters the grammars of sand, root trench,
black beetle.
He knows a hundred homes:
the plain wild with henbane,
the loam over which thornapples
hang their spiked pods,
the peat's assassins tread.
He survives minor floods like a covered boat.
He speaks the tongues of potash and manure.

Where fate marks him,
he answers with healing.
A folk Osiris, hacked into pieces,
he rises whole, and yearly.
Burial is his beginning.
His eyes make light of the dark.

SLUGS

Always the last guests
at the banquet, arriving
from old cisterns and plant-heaps
long after dark,
you mark your trails
neatly, wandering laces of slime
of interest to crickets and house cats.

I watch you, the greatest four inches long,
tigered like flatworms or pike,
nose the round bits of potato
into evening's senescence.

I admire your delicate eyestalks,
the fluid contentment of your bodies,
the way you go back where you came from
saying nothing, gleaming
and muscular as silence.

CROCKIES

Time's nest, I found them in the garden,
clutched like a toothed bird's fossil brood,
clay curling over their pocked moony curves
like a lover's mourning fingers
over death's closed eyes.
Rousted from dirt's seeping keep,
they paled in sun, drying.

Five of them, like the knuckles
of a drowned and flood-hewn queen.
Disarticulate. Strewn.

I cleaned them, on toward evening,
displayed them on the basement
window sill. Rollers
arrested, stared at by
the blind eye
of my foundation.

Once openings out of the earth,
palmed by a potter's moist hands,
thumbed in fun by boys
wrenched to a bitter darkness,
in an alien now
they scab and crack,
night harvest.

And now they are five eyes,
two men's and a monster's,
blank and inward
as secrets
worth keeping
secret.

AT THE EDGE OF AGNES

Above her northeast steady roar
I heard all day the roof-rain
off my snake-run trailer:
old clang-handled bucket
at the corner
where the runoff foamed
a green head thick
as timothy gone to seed.

An Ohio hurricane:
rare as bobcats in the hollows.
Through that trial
of scud and blow
I watched my dog
pace wall to wall
then wedge herself
beneath the rattling table
where my pencils rolled
like timber in a flume.
I watched the sumacs snap
their greenwood by the garden,
watched, and tried to think,
tried to write it.
Nothing came
but thunder's boomed confusion
from the ridge.

Then sunlight, brittle,
burst upon the wreckage:
several poplars down,
the garden beaten
to a pox of clay-fouled ponds.

Two days later,
that roof-rain, heated by the sun,
simmered in the bucket,

already rich with the seething commas
of mosquito larvae.
For three weeks then
I sat in humming, droning shade,
sweating out the long sentence
of survival.
Rash roses blooming
on my wrists and neck,
I tried, stalled, tried again,
labored at by storm's strange leavings —
grammars of wild light and heat and thriving,
a blood-hungry punctuation.

HOUSE CATS

Hatched from the blackest eggs of night,
asquawl on the stones of the suburbs,
they live to sneak beyond porch lights
toward the delicate warblings of wrens
dreaming in innocent shrubs.
Expert stalkers
of the passionate, beautiful small —
shrew, field mouse, mantis —
they hunt merely to maul
with a rapid and finicky disgust.
Regularly, they eat their own hair.

Nor will they answer to a name.
They want to be mysterious,
like Egypt,
who, to rid herself of their plague,
entombed them with her dead.
They want to be anonymous,
and to steal, like government spies or assassins,
through darkness forever,
silent,
sharpening their clever knives.

MIDAFTERNOON, JULY

The hawk of fever
rises steadily
above the stick-dry ridge:
scrub and pitch pines
drop their needles
on the turtles in the rocks.

Fire is everywhere and nervous,
waiting for the farmer's misplaced pipe,
for the boy's dropped matches
in the hayloft,
for the passing driver's spark.

The jug of water
I just drew
sits sweating
on the counter.

An Arctic Skipper
beats itself to tinder
against the kitchen screen.

LATE KILL

Fifteen, my dog
gave up the deer chase
early her last summer.
Come back nearly lame each dawn
from instinct's mournful treason,
she flopped loose and winded
on the porch floor
in her first of many daily shades
to gnaw her thorn and smilax bonds.
But every afternoon,
when the skillet
of the county road had cooled,
she rose and wandered off again,
ears back,
to lurk among
the roadside berry canes.

One day, she brought it back.
Small, a two-pound yearling,
slack and dripping blood,
it looked the nadir of all groundhog
when she dropped it in the pigweed,
paced two times
around it,
then stretched out
to start her feed.
At first I doubted.
She labored at the tail-end,
snapping claw, leg-bone,
the gristly bridge of hip.
But hide and all, she
ate half that groundhog
in an hour.
Her eyes glazed
weirdly as she rested.

Mine too seemed then to drift off-center:
in the green haze of the
heaving afternoon
the sumacs blurred,
a reeking fizz of flies
swarmed close,
something bloody
gurgled in my throat.

Then Act Two
commenced, the body
still on stage.
She got a dew-claw
deep into the shoulder
of the thing,
ripped expertly
till the slathered bag
exploded.
A clot of fresh work
glinted.

Another hour passed.
I could not stand
too surely on the porch,
leaned sweating
on the door post.
Tiny finches, green-gold,
sparked and smoldered
in the air before my eyes.
Just the head was left.

Then she stood,
belly hanging like a broken mattress,
and scratched a hole
the size of half an osage-orange.
She dropped the smeared knob in.
She struggled up the steps,

sneering sidelong at me
for a moment,
and lowered snout
to drink loudly from the bucket.

That night, as usual,
she slept beneath my bed.
Five times I stirred
to dismal rumblings
that quivered her old flanks.
Five times I nearly drifted off again,
but lay, suspended, in that mid-place
neither sleep nor waking,
neither hell nor heaven,
where wren lies wrapped in blacksnake,
where shrew dishevels in fox's maw,
where thought darkens like a bloodstain
spreading on the floor.

MAN WITH A DAMAGED LEG

Sat on the broken porch
in a great fin of shade,
buckled roof a manta
floating the upward blue fathoms.

"Coral Sea," he said, spitting
Mail Pouch, rubbing his thigh.
"Hurts every summer the worse."
Children watching, eyes

opening and closing, pale valves.
Hawks screaming down the reefs
of ridge-edge. Out on the road,
a shark-gray mastiff whining.

OLD FISHING LINES

By day you see them,
festoons of flood-spun ten-pound test,
draped like nets from
river willows gnarled and stunted as bonsai.

They have a delicacy of curve
like the wings of dragonflies
and swallows.

They have come back
from dim marvels of sinkholes,
the wreckage of cities,
flood's ungodly gutturals.

Now, they fray at their ends,
try their thinness on the wind,
as if risen from darkness
they fully must break into feather,
testing for flight the bright air.

TOWARD THE END OF A LONG RIDE

Day ends miles before
the place we flee to
sprouts its signs
that tell us nothing.

Their gaudy nightglo greens
loom in our headlights
like floating displaced meadows
over fogpatch, stuttered lines,

red flicks of a fox's eyes.
Tired and hungry, we swerve
wildly round and round
the mountains, past lakes

that hold old homesteads
at their bottoms as a man's
sleep holds old dreams.
Names are all obscured.

And always, it grows later.
We nod off on the curves.
Only the berm's gravel
clattering rocker panels

wakes us. We pull over where
a sycamore leans cross-creek.
We jangle beer cans with
each step, descend to find a rock,

sit down. Above, the car
ticks, cooling. A few frogs
call across the dark: *wheep
wheep racket racket: wheep.*

One star settles on a branch.
It is grandma's cancer,
father's heart attack,
the blank eye of a wrecked owl

dying. Then something slips
downstream before us, quiet as
a poacher who boats his oars
near where he wants to trap,

who hardly breathes but
chains his steel tools
to a shattered stump with a clank
and lash as final as all

slaughter, then slowly
wedges back against a thwart
to wait, thinks nothing,
does not speak, goes nowhere.

Eyes heavy, we see it
slump and settle, turn a vagueness
like a face toward where we sit.
It smiles. We know it. Now we sleep.

HAT ON A ROCK

1
Again it is August.
The few birds left
wither into autumn,
their faint songs
clipped and frugal
in the heat.

Nor is my voice strong.
I sit beneath a broken cottonwood,
my body sluggish,
wearily stale,
backwater.

Old logs, a spit
of broken bricks,
a few dulled lumps
of glass:
within their
shoring
I turn in, eddy
slowly on myself,
go nowhere.

2
Who has left
his hat here on this rock,
red polka dots on gray,
bill warped and tattered,
stained with bait and whiskey?

Did he too have no name?
Did he too hear a voice
in this slow green
moaning,
slowly stand,
slip in,
and answer?

Maybe no one will know.
But maybe some unpainted dredge,
laboring upstream
in the diesel mists
of dead summer,
works, even now,
the dark silt
of his becoming.

ROOT FENCE

Like the wreckage of mastodons
and mammoths, jumbled megatheriums
long unfleshed by time and wind and sun,
their bones heaped helter-skelter in the lurchings
of landscape toward geology,
my neighbor's strange fence —
roots of downed oak, beech, and poplar —
snags shadows in its wild confusions,
chiaroscuro uncertainties
on a simple hill in Ohio.

Nothing like it lines another place
around the county: split-rail, picket,
post-and-wire elsewhere reticulate the land
that wants to drop off toward its ancient sea-floors
but cannot for all their plotted holding.
Instead, shadows straight as chains or rods
benignly lie upon the timothy and oats,
shadows measured, safe as sills.
But the doors that plunge to
darkness throughout the root fence

will not be entered safely. Humid
passages to regions previous and lost,
where toothed beasts large as sheds
thrust tusks and horns upwards through
a wilderness of soil, open everywhere
along its weed-shagged length.
It leaks a living dusk
more extensive than the night,
moon igniting dim mosaics
of hide, hoof, unblinking eye,
glintings of an old, neanderthalic ice.

But some are drawn to its tangled brooding
on the ridge, find something long forgotten
since the conquest of the land, the
quelling of old demons. Weary
of noon's unceasing brilliance, enslaved
to sunlight's trite productions,
they long for wildness never tamed,
for a night as deep as time,
so pass by here, alone, to glory, quiet,
in a kind of sacred terror, thinking
"It is right sometimes to draw
these things up from the dark,
to haunt the light."

IN THE CEMETERY

Unheralded, unaudienced, earth's blatant
show goes on: rube and upstart thistles
loaf inside the gate, daylilies spread like
gaudy easy marks before a leaning tent of broom sedge,
slick grass snake illusionists loop familiar names
that dissolve and reappear
across old headstones.

I come here to commune
with nothing, with that pleasant silent entropy
that falls, as gradually as decay,
into the deaths of all the busy.

But sulphur butterflies flag the fox-graped air,
a jay waves above a locust, shrieking,
then dives daredevil toward the creek.
Katydids and greenfrogs hurdy-gurdy day
to a steady beep and heaving.
From every gone heart under stone
explodes the clown-dance of creation.
From every roadside ditch
chugs and bubbles life's cheap beer
transformed by masked mad chemists
in ancient japes
that never fail to work —
here, the poltroon toad,
here, the spangled skink,
here, tough lichens making Cheshire grins of growth
in their wild, pratfall survival.

SHORE GLASS, CINCINNATI

Here the common river, clogged with
coal dust and the red-clay sand of brick,
low stones smeared with shad-silt,
perch-bladder, reeking skin of mudcat,
delivers its surprising jewels
to the battered concrete on its banks.

All day, boys come down
with sacks to glean
this treasure —
bromo bottles shattered
in the Pennsylvania uplands,
then roared down-flood,
smoothed to deep sapphire
in the river's lapidary tumble;
Ohio bottle bottoms
shaped like Hopewell gods and totems;
jugs and moonshine jars
slivered bright as mica
in the wrack.

Watching these boys
intent in mud and stones,
I see an opal haze surround them,
see the instinct to collect
all that flashes, glitters,
gathers light to glinting,
curve in upon them like a lens
of Byzantine enamel,
and I think of bower birds
who set blue stones
among their chapels in the forest,
as if to make connect
the fury in their blood —

to court and mate,
to deck, dapple,
be dazzled by world's brilliance —
with the daily service
of the elegance of life,
the rich increase
of beauty's million species.

NIGHT ANATOMY

There is a dark bird
in her arm
that needs to kill.
She hangs a heavy purse
upon it,
keeps it down.
But still her hand
is like a hawk's head,
hard knot
drawn out to hook.

When she sleeps,
that long arm hanging
over bed's edge
beats its wings,
aching to break loose.

All bodies are strangers
at times, grown
dire and reckless at night:
the philosopher's skull
like a bludgeon,
the virgin's small hands
like assassins,
the President's feet
like dead roots
turned up by machines
in old graveyards.

FROST

At the creek
a night of hard edges,
glass leaves shattered
over stone.
I am No Shadow,
trailing my ghost
of breath.
I step over scattered
stars,
pale asters of ice,
moon's nails
strewn where water
found them
and stopped.

LISTENING TO VIVALDI WHILE WATCHING
STARLINGS ABOVE THE RAILROAD

This music has its wings:
the deep bassoon lifts
itself, rises
above the damp earth of its tones
to fly.
       I ride it
out into December.
Ohio falls from me,
a clatter of arrowheads,
mica, jawbones.

Now I am wrapped
in a pelt of black air
and shout down
to the thistles
in tongues.

FALSE SPRING

Day made clearly
on the warming ridge
that dawn: one bee,
thawed from comb crystals,
droned across the dulled
ruts of the garden,
swerved windward
toward the pines.
Sun stirred a seedling
warmth along the hillside.

He walked downridge
to Brown's Run, whip-snake
of glass frosted
through the hollow.
Beneath a thinning lens
of ice he watched
minnows magnified
to bass. Light
lifted stumps
from season-long shadows,
rocks from hillsfoot spills.

Then the weather
toughened, sky
clouded, wind
keened its flinty
edges: slashed leaves
whirled in it like ghosts.

Sleet's nails fastened
sky to land. Trees,
black risers walled
stand to stand with wind,

groaned under gray weight,
loaded silver.

Nothing listened
as his heart stalled,
grown hard again as rose quartz
in its clumsy sled of rime.

STONE

What crack traps sunlight
by this river
lives immensely,
widens with that heat
and water's dampness,
spews willows from its heart
and holds the heron
in its shade.

After many years
the boulder splits, kin to sand
but giant,
and begins its
endless fission.

Listen:
in late evenings
stone is dark noise,
level with the water.

SPARROW HAWK

Alive above the freeway,
it is knot, storm, pounder:
a fist of sight
clenched to hammer movement
into food.

Walking home from teaching,
I am not living
in its world: pity
for the fieldmouse
stirring in
the roadcut broom sedge
far below
disinvolves me
from the plain hard fact
of hunger.

But in its sudden stooping
from the highline,
all the books explode
inside my briefcase;
heroes fade
into a haze;
words hang empty
as the wire
that hawk has plunged from:

For a moment, I am certain
I must live among claw
and splintered rib,
must taste
a thousand species of splashed blood,
must thrust my head
deep into world's
soft guts
and tear them.

ONE FOR MAGNAVOX AND NIETZSCHE

"It's still. By God, it doesn't move."
— what Galileo might have said

The click and clink of junk,
trash-tintinnabulation,
crash, crack, cleave and splitting,
fracture, breakdown, everything nearly obsolete
or obsolete completely,
disrepair, disorder,
chaos entire
and unrepentant,
un-self-effacing,
proud of itself, a raving
disinheritance of atoms from their forms,
molecules amuck,
the wristwatch jimmied, gears asprawl
and dangling,
the artificial eye askew,
the gaze akimbo,
the world disjointed, unarticulated,
great busy intersections rank with nonsense
of machines,
and beneath it all, pale
squirm and whimper,
mauled to disappearing,
that huge and bearded serviceman
of world,
the Great Repairman tool-less,
fingering, as if a prayer bead
or his last-ditch dime,
the wrong-sized bolt
he tried to fix it with.
Good help, these days, is hard to find.

POSSIBLE DEBRIS

What approaches feels like winter.
Clumps of broom sedge tremble in the wind,
seed this stalled earth to a future
then mulch themselves with themselves.

In the cold sun's sparse light,
motes, racemes, down of thistle,
slips of splintered burrs
spin vagrant on a wandering air.

The smoke of old fires hazes
Dearth Ridge all the way to Graysville.
Along the roads, tines of rusted
lilies clash themselves to ash.

Everywhere I look, world falls loose,
collapses: barn doors sprung and piled
against the inside bends of creeks,
scattered bones of foxes

runing wasted hardpan, the last
lean ears of field corn deranged
like yellow teeth across the ground.
Everywhere debris.

But what is possible will come:
the leafless poplar on the bare west ridge
still holds its life within itself,
rooted deep enough to keep.

I relinquish, too: drop my leaves, to see.
And in this pitch and mix of ending, in this flux
and shattering, I bide to find new growth,
the sudden spring-and-fit of thing to thing.